St. Francis

(a short biography)

• • •

KATHLEEN M. CARROLL

Franciscan
MEDIA
Cincinnati, Ohio

Scripture passages have been taken from *New Revised Standard Version Bible*, copyright ©1989 by the Division of Christian Education of the National Council of the Churches of Christ in the U.S.A., and used by permission. All rights reserved.

Cover and book design by Mark Sullivan
Cover image © PhotoXpress | Ioannis Syrigos

ISBN 978-1-61636-521-9

Copyright ©2012, Kathleen M. Carroll. All rights reserved.
Published by Franciscan Media
28 W. Liberty St.
Cincinnati, OH 45202
www.FranciscanMedia.org

Printed in the United States of America.
Printed on acid-free paper.

12 13 14 15 16   5 4 3 2 1

Contents

Introduction

If you've only heard of one saint, chances are it is St. Francis of Assisi. His international popularity hasn't waned in eight hundred years. In fact, if Francis was a man born ahead of his time, in many ways his time is now.

His profound love of all created things was the source of his reputation as an animal lover. One legend tells how he saved a small town from a fierce wolf. He called the beast "Brother Wolf," and persuaded him to make peace with the villagers. The wolf would no longer prey on the town's livestock or citizens; in return, the people would give him food.

Another story tells of Francis stopping in a field to preach to the birds. They gathered around him and kept silent while he spoke. They burst into song when he urged them to praise God. Francis called them "my little sisters" and told his followers to imitate the birds in their joy, their humility, and their trust in providence.

Long before sorting your recyclables was in vogue, Francis had a deep connection with the earth. He saw himself as just one part of creation. The earth and the air, fire and water, birds and beasts were all part of the same glorious creation. They were his brothers and sisters, not mere objects to be dominated, tolerated, or ignored. God created the world, and Francis saw that it was very good.

Pope John Paul II declared Francis "patron saint of ecology" in 1979, and the U.S. bishops praised Francis in their document *Renewing the Earth*. "Safeguarding creation requires us to live responsibly in it, rather than managing creation as though we are outside it," they wrote. Francis had that insight long before climate change became a catchphrase.

Francis also was a man of peace. In a time of holy wars, he set out to win glory as a martyr. Instead he met with a Muslim sultan whose faith was so sincere that Francis dismissed the popular idea that Christians had a monopoly on earnestly seeking God. It was a startling message for his time, and no less startling for ours.

This little book will give you a glimpse into the life of that man behind the birdbath, that wise man who has so much to say to our age.

Favored Son

In 1181, just eleven years after the martyrdom of Thomas Becket, sixty years after the death of Omar Khayyam, and thirty after the birth of gothic architecture, a modestly wealthy couple in a small Italian town welcomed a son and heir. His pious mother, Pica, had him baptized Giovanni—John; his practical father, Pietro Bernardone, changed the child's name to Francesco upon returning from a business trip to France.

Assisi was caught in a web of political intrigue that plagued the twelfth century. An ancient Roman walled city, it was in its own tiny way a picture of the upheaval that raged across Europe. The feudal system of the post-Roman centuries still held sway, but fiefdoms were beginning to lose some of the stability—and stagnation—that colored much of the Dark Ages. As Western

1

Christianity went to war against a powerful Muslim presence in the East, the loss of favored sons and hereditary titles made for easy pickings among the once-powerful families back home. The experience of war, the exposure to other (arguably more advanced) cultures, and the discovery of new goods meant that even those who returned home were changed. A large house with enough acres and servants to sustain a dynasty was no longer enough for the ambitious. Knowing how quickly war can change fortunes and knowing how to wage war proved too tempting a combination and neither land nor loyalty had the enduring value it once possessed. In a time when everything could change, everything did.

Assisi had been a papal protectorate until its citizens stormed the stronghold at the top of the hill overlooking the city (the Rocca Maggiore) in 1189. It was then under the control of the Ghibellines, a political faction perpetually at war with the Guelphs, who ruled the nearby town of Perugia. Ancestral lineage still mattered—those who could trace their origins to royalty could expect some support in their efforts to assert power. The Church, too, was a political machine—few rulers could hold power without some seal of approval from Rome. And Italy—a united nation—was not even yet a dream of its people. The peninsula was carved into constantly shifting city-states, papal states, and loosely allied territories.

If war was once again showing its talent for creating power, it had competition. The Crusades, which were on-again, off-again affairs, established new trade routes with the East. The changes in social structure in Europe meant that more people had goods and gold to trade. A rising merchant class could buy respectability—even titles—from feudal lords and social mobility became a real possibility for some. It was no longer inevitable that one would die in the same social class (likely the same house) where one was born. Both war and trade were risky and both promised wild rewards for those who were successful.

It was into this world of uncertainty and upheaval that the man we know as Francis of Assisi was born. Some children seem out of place from the start. These are the ones who grow up never quite fitting into the world, or perhaps drastically changing it, or both. Francis was not such a child. He was very much of his world, of his age. He was known to his companions as the sort of man who could not only abide in such an uncertain world, but positively thrived on it. His earliest biographer, Thomas of Celano, a writer whose reverence for the man Francis would become cannot be overstated, was candid about those early years:

> In the city of Assisi, which lies at the edge of the Spoleto valley, there was a man by the name of Francis, who from his earliest years was brought up by his parents proud of spirit, in accordance with the vanity of the world; and imitating their wretched life and habits for a long time, he became even more vain and proud....
>
> These are the wretched circumstances among which the man whom we venerate today as a saint, for he is truly a saint, lived in his youth; and almost up to the twenty-fifth year of his age, he squandered and wasted his time miserably. Indeed, he outdid all his contemporaries in vanities and he came to be a promoter of evil and was more abundantly zealous for all kinds of foolishness. He was the admiration of all and strove to outdo the rest in the pomp of vainglory, in jokes, in strange doings, in idle and useless talk, in songs, in soft and flowing garments, for he was

very rich, not however avaricious but prodigal, not a hoarder of money but a squanderer of his possessions, a cautious business man but a very unreliable steward. On the other hand, he was a very kindly person, easy and affable, even making himself foolish because of it; for because of these qualities many ran after him, doers of evil and promoters of crime.

This hardly sounds like the sort of man who would one day be a saint, but it does recall some of the more sordid stories of irresponsible trust-fund children of our own day. Francis's father was a shrewd businessman; he exploited the new possibilities in trade to great profit. His razor-sharp instinct for advancement extended to his family. He wanted the best of everything for his wife and seven children. As a cloth merchant, he made sure they were always dressed in the finest fabrics and the latest fashions. His generosity meant that Francis always had money to treat his friends to lavish parties. And Pietro wanted more—a knighthood for Francis, a title for the family. Pietro was no short-sighted money-grubber: He deftly managed the chaos of his day and meant to use his skill to establish a dynasty.

Francis, this vain, pleasure-loving, charming son, embraced the task his father set before him. If he looked good in brocade and velvet, how much better would he look in armor astride a warhorse?

Warrior

Assisi was a typical hill town. The poor lived in the valley below, outside the walls. The ruling class lived at the top (the Rocca Maggiore had been both fort and palace in its day). Everyone one else sorted themselves out somewhere in between. Life outside the city walls was risky. Criminals were tireless and inventive and a civil police force had been a rarity since the time of the Romans. Lepers roamed the lanes, begging for the alms upon which their lives depended, ringing bells to warn others away. And war was like a thunderstorm—you might get some warning if a particularly nasty one was brewing, but you might equally find yourself surprised by an afternoon shower.

Most windows in the city looked toward the Umbrian Valley below and to a slightly larger town, Perugia, on the next hilltop about ten miles away. In Francis's day, Perugia was controlled by a competing political party—an ideal situation for a young man bent on glory. War was always just an hour away.

When he was about twenty, Francis took one of the many opportunities his circumstances afforded him and went to battle against Perugia. No specific cause was cited (nor was any needed); it is clear that Francis viewed this as a necessary first rung on his chosen career ladder. And, though he did not display a particular knack for warfare, it suited him admirably. *The Legend of the Three Companions* tells us:

> During a year of war between Perugia and Assisi Francis was captured together with many of his fellow citizens and was taken to prison in Perugia. Because of his distinguished bearing, he was put among the nobles. One day his companions were especially downhearted, but Francis, who was naturally cheerful, far from appearing sad, seemed almost to be enjoying himself. One of his fellow prisoners reproached him as a fool for looking happy at being in prison. Francis answered: "Is that what you think of me? The day will come when I shall be honored by the whole world." Among his companions there was one who had

injured a fellow prisoner, for which reason all the others wished
to cold-shoulder him; but Francis alone refused and urged them
to follow his example. After a year, on the conclusion of peace,
he, with the other prisoners, returned to Assisi.

All we know of Francis's role in this episode is that he was fabu-
lously dressed and equipped, annoyingly cheerful in prison, and
lonely in his willingness to forgive the odd man out. He seems to
have been satisfied with trading a year of his life as a prisoner of
war for the boost it would offer his military career.

While no one suggests that the experience was a holiday, writ-
ers close to the event report that Francis found war to be pretty
much what he expected—a risky enterprise that could win him
knighthood and the wealth and honor that accompanied that
status. Indeed, he was well prepared to meet war at the next
possible opportunity. As *The Legend* relates:

A few years later an Assisian nobleman was planning to start for
Apulia on a military expedition which he hoped would bring him
money and honors. Hearing of this, Francis was fired with the
wish to accompany him and to get knighted by a certain Count

Gentile. He prepared magnificent equipment; and, though his fellow citizen was a nobleman, Francis was by far the more extravagant of the two.

Francis's father had groomed his son for great things and Francis seems to have taken this to heart. His comment to his fellow prisoners in Perugia hints at this. On the eve of this next military adventure, he began to understand that his destiny was not simply the result of his father's machinations or the good fortune of being born into a rapidly changing world. His future was so grand that it had been ordained by God.

He was absorbed in this plan and keen to set out, when one night he was visited by the Lord, who, seeing him so bent on honor and glory, drew him to himself by means of a vision. While Francis was asleep, a man appeared who called him by name and led him into a vast and pleasant palace in which the walls were hung with glittering coats of mail, shining bucklers, and all the weapons and armor of warriors. Francis was delighted, and reflecting on what could be the meaning of all this, he asked for whom the splendid arms and beautiful palace were intended; and he received the answer that they were for him and his knights.

On awaking, Francis rose gleefully, thinking, after the manner of worldlings (for he had not yet tasted the spirit of God) that he was destined to become a magnificent prince and that the vision was prophetic of great prosperity. What he had seen spurred him on to start for Apulia and to get himself knighted in the following of Count Gentile. His glee was such that people, in surprise, asked the reason of his delight and received the answer: "I know that I shall become a great prince."

If Francis was known for being naturally cheerful, this vision made him giddy. The Western world was still Catholic; faith in God was as near a universal constant as that world possessed. It would not have been unusual to look for some divine guidance in planning one's life and receiving a vision was not a matter for skepticism. Among cynical men of war, though, talk of visions would do nothing to enhance Francis's well-crafted image of a warrior. Though encouraged by the vision, he shared his confidence, but made no mention of its source.

As it happens, this was a wise choice. Since his vision had told him everything he wanted to hear, Francis accepted it as genuine and embraced it wholeheartedly. His joy was short-lived, though. *The Legend of the Three Companions* explains:

Now it happened that, after the start for Apulia, Francis felt unwell on arriving at Spoleto; and thinking with apprehension about the journey, he went to bed; but, half asleep, he heard a voice calling and asking him whither he was bound. He replied, telling of his plan. Then he, who had previously appeared to him in sleep, spoke these words:

"Who do you think can best reward you, the Master or the servant?"

"The Master," answered Francis.

"Then why do you leave the Master for the servant, the rich Lord for the poor man?"

Francis replied: "O Lord, what do you wish me to do?" "Return to your own place," he was bidden, "and you will be told what to do. You must interpret your vision in a different sense. The arms and palace you saw are intended for other knights than those you had in mind; and your principality too will be of another order."

Francis awoke and began to turn all this over in his mind. After the first vision he had been in a transport of delight, filled with desires for worldly prosperity; but this one left him puzzled and perplexed. He thought about it so intensely that he slept no more that night. Immediately at daybreak he started back towards Assisi in glad expectation that God, who had shown him the vision, would soon reveal his will for the future. Francis now waited to be guided by him for the salvation of his soul. His mind was changed and he gave up all thought of going to Apulia.

Francis was still his father's son. He still wanted those knights, that palace, the reward of a great master. His vision told him that he could not achieve great things by serving the minor nobility. He did not know where his future lay, but he knew that his current course was taking him in the wrong direction. He went home to await his destiny.

chapter
three

Waiting

For a young man whose life had been so meticulously planned for him—first by his father, and then later by his military commanders—waiting in limbo must have been a profound challenge for Francis. He returned to his family, his hometown, his old friends, but he was never quite the same. He seemed always to be waiting, listening, tuned in to some strange frequency, awaiting further directions. When inspiration came, as it always does to those who wait patiently for it, Francis responded. Whatever idea popped into his head enchanted him and became his marching orders.

Though he wanted to rush headlong into his destiny, Francis had no idea where to begin. He would do something great, but what? He would serve God, the greatest of all masters, but how?

The Legend of the Three Companions tells of this twilight time:

> Soon after Francis had returned to Assisi, his companions elected him king of the revels, and gave him a free hand to spend what he liked in the preparation of a sumptuous banquet as he had often done on other occasions. After the feast they left the house and started off singing through the streets. Francis' companions were leading the way; and he, holding his wand of office, followed them at a little distance. Instead of singing, he was listening very attentively. All of a sudden the Lord touched his heart, filling it with such surpassing sweetness that he could neither speak nor move. He could only feel and hear this overwhelming sweetness which detached him so completely from all other physical sensations that, as he said later, had he been cut to pieces on the spot he could not have moved.
>
> When his companions looked around, they saw him in the distance and turned back. To their amazement they saw that he was transformed into another man, and they asked him: "What were you thinking of? Why didn't you follow us? Were you thinking of getting married?"

Francis answered in a clear voice: "You are right: I was thinking of wooing the noblest, richest, and most beautiful bride ever seen." His friends laughed at him saying he was a fool and did not know what he was saying; in reality he had spoken by a divine inspiration. The bride was none other than that form of true religion which he embraced; and which, above any other is noble, rich, and beautiful in its poverty.

From that hour he began to consider himself as naught and to despise all those things he had formerly cherished; but he still did so imperfectly, not being as yet entirely detached from worldly vanities. He gradually withdrew from the tumult of earthly things and applied himself secretly to receive Jesus Christ into his soul with that pearl of great price which he so desired as to be willing to sell all he possessed in order to gain it. To this end he often hid himself from the eyes of deceitful men and withdrew to pray in secret, incited to do so by the same sweetness in his heart which took possession of him with increasing frequency, drawing him apart to pray far from all public meeting places.

He was already a benefactor of the poor, but from this time onwards he resolved never to refuse alms to anyone who begged in God's name; but rather to give more willingly and abundantly than ever before. If a poor person begged of him when he was far from home, he would always give him money, if possible; when he had none he would give his belt or buckle; or, if he had not even these, he would find a hiding place and, taking off his shirt, give it to the beggar for love of God. In addition to this, he was most liberal in buying vases and other objects pertaining to the service and adornment of churches and he sent them secretly to poor priests.

Sometimes it happened that Francis remained in the house alone with his mother while his father was away on business; on these occasions he would heap the table with loaves, both for dinner and supper, as though for the whole family. One day his mother asked him why he prepared so much bread, and he replied that he wished to distribute the loaves to those in need because he had promised always to give alms to anyone who begged from him in God's name. His mother loved him more than her other children, and therefore she let him have his way in these things; but she observed all he did, and often secretly marveled at it.

In former years he had so enjoyed the company of his friends that he was always ready to join them; they only had to call and Francis would leave the table and be off, having barely tasted his food, and leaving his parents greatly distressed at such untimely haste. Now, however, his whole heart was entirely bent on seeing, hearing, and attending to the poor; and he gave them generous alms in the name of God.

He was still living in the world though already greatly changed by divine grace; and sometimes the longing seized him for a place where, as an unknown stranger, he could give his own clothes to some beggar, taking the beggar's miserable rags in exchange and setting out himself to beg for love of God.

At this time he happened to go to Rome on pilgrimage, and in the church of Saint Peter he noticed that many people left what seemed to him very inadequate offerings. He said to himself: "Surely, the greatest honor is due to the Prince of the Apostles; how then can some folk leave such meager alms in the church where his body rests?" Full of fervor he took a handful of money from his purse and threw it in through a grating in the altar; the coins made such a clatter that those present heard it and were greatly astonished at such munificence.

Francis then left the church, and on the steps before the entrance a number of beggars were asking for money from those who came and went. Francis quietly borrowed the clothes of one of these beggars, changing into them from his own; and, dressed in rags, he stood on the steps with the others, asking for alms in French, a language he delighted to speak, though he did not know it very well.

After a while he changed back into his own garments and returned to Assisi, devoutly praying that the Lord would show him the right path. At home he told no one of his secret, and turned to God who alone was his never failing guide; neither did he ask advice of anyone except sometimes of the Bishop of Assisi. He looked in vain in those around him for that real poverty which he desired above all earthly things and in which he wanted to live and die.

One day while Francis was praying fervently to God, he received an answer. "O Francis, if you want to know my will, you must hate and despise all that which hitherto your body has loved and desired to possess. Once you begin to do this, all that formerly seemed sweet and pleasant to you will become bitter and unbearable; and instead, the things that formerly made you shudder will bring you great sweetness and content." Francis was divinely comforted and greatly encouraged by these words. Then one day, as he was riding near Assisi, he met a leper. He had always felt an overpowering horror of these sufferers; but making a great effort, he conquered his aversion, dismounted, and, in giving the leper a coin, kissed his hand. The leper then gave him the kiss of peace, after which Francis remounted his horse and rode on his way. From that day onwards he mortified himself increasingly until, through God's grace, he won a complete victory.

Some days later he took a large sum of money to the leper hospital, and gathering all the inmates together, he gave them alms, kissing each of their hands. Formerly he could neither touch or even look at lepers, but when he left them on that day, what had been so repugnant to him had really and truly been turned into something pleasant. Indeed, his previous aversion to lepers had been so strong, that, besides being incapable of looking at them, he would not even approach the places where they lived. And if by chance he happened to pass anywhere near their dwellings or to see one of the lepers, even though he was moved to give them an alms through some intermediate person, he would nevertheless turn his face away and hold his nose. But, strengthened by God's grace, he was enabled to obey the command and to love what he had hated and to abhor what he had hitherto wrongfully loved. In consequence of this he became such a friend to the lepers that, as he himself declared in his Testament, he lived with them and served them with loving eagerness.

After his visits to the lepers Francis changed for the better. Taking with him a favorite Assisian companion of his own age, he used to seek out remote and solitary spots, telling his friend that he had found a great treasure. This pleased the other young man, who followed Francis gladly whenever he called. They went frequently to a cave near Assisi, and while the friend, on the lookout for treasure, remained outside, Francis went in alone, and, with his heart full of a new, unaccustomed fervor, he prayed to God his Father. He wished that none should know what he did in the cave but God alone, to whom he prayed assiduously to show him how to find the heavenly treasure.

When the Devil saw Francis' good beginning, he tried ingeniously to turn him from it by suggestions of fright or disgust. In Assisi there was a humpbacked and deformed woman; and the Devil recalled her to Francis' mind with the threat that, unless he turned from the good he had embarked on, he would free her from her deformity and cast it upon him. Francis, however, was strong in the Lord and, heedless of the Devil's threats, he prayed devoutly in the cave that God would direct his steps into the right way. He endured great mental anguish and could find no rest for he was searching how he could put into practice what was in his heart. Importunate ideas came and went and greatly worried and distressed him. His heart was aglow with divine fire, and even outwardly he could not hide the new ardor which was taking possession of him and filling him with repentance for his past grave sins. He found no satisfaction in evil whether past or present; but he also lacked confidence in his own capacity for avoiding evil in the future. When he emerged from the cave and rejoined his friend, this inner struggle had so changed him as to make him appear a different man.

One day while Francis was fervently imploring God's mercy, the Lord revealed to him that he would shortly be taught what he was to do. From that moment he was so full of joy that, beside himself for gladness, he would let fall occasional words of his secret for men to hear. This happened in spite of his habitual caution; for he did not speak openly and merely declared that he no longer wished to go to Apulia but would do great things in his own land. His companions noticed how changed he was; and indeed his heart was already far from them, even though occasionally he accepted their company. They tried to probe into his mind and again asked whether he was thinking of marrying, and as before he answered in a figure of speech: "I shall bring home a bride, more beautiful, richer, and nobler than any you have ever seen."

This dreamy, distracted Francis worried his friends. He acted like a young man in love, but this eligible bachelor, this "king of revels," did not follow the steps of courtship. If he had a bride in mind, who could it be? And, though his friends knew that he was keeping secrets, what would they have thought of his dressing as a beggar, kissing lepers, seeking solitude while he waited for God?

Francis had always been generous, but now he was seeking out the poor rather than showering his friends with gifts. Thomas of Celano says: "When he was approached by beggars, he was not content merely to give what he had—he wanted to give his whole self to them. At times he took off his clothes and gave them away, or ripped or tore pieces from them, if he had nothing else at hand." He had always been cheerful, but now he wavered between the vacant ecstasy of a man in love and the stern self-criticism of a man who feels unworthy of love. Without a plotted course before him, without an image to emulate, Francis grew into a more vibrant version of himself. He was wealthy and popular and people were willing to tolerate his new strangeness for an occasional glimpse of the old Francis—the one who knew his place in the world, the one who made all their own ambitions seem attractive, attainable, and honorable.

But Francis's greatest secret was that he did not know his place in the world. The things that once allured him—money, power, fame—were inconsequential to him now. He wanted only to be carried away by his visions, by a thousand tiny inspirations that drew him closer to God. He began this period of limbo waiting for the directions to his destiny, to the great reward that awaited him. He ended it wanting only to serve God, without thought of reward. Once he understood why he wanted to serve, knowing how to serve was certain to follow.

chapter four

The Vision

Some of Francis's biographers oversimplify his early life. "There was a dapper young man," they tell us, "who one day had a vision that changed his life." This does Francis a disservice. His "conversion," as it's often called, was not instant and it was not easy. He was born and raised in a devout family; doubtless he thought that he was doing his Christian duty simply by following the path his family and friends laid out for him. Once that notion was taken from him, he had nothing to take its place.

Though it is still somewhat true today, people in Francis's day were best identified by what they did. Whether one was a soldier, a merchant, a cleric, or a serf, this was far more than a job or even a career—it was a vocation. While we might be tolerant of young people who try their hands at several trades in an effort to "find themselves," this was a rarity in the Middle Ages. One was what one did and if one did nothing, well, one was nothing. A son of wealth, Francis was able to coast longer than most, but it was becoming clear to all that Francis was no longer pursuing a knighthood, took only slight interest in his father's business, and did not even fully embrace the rich playboy lifestyle offered to him.

The fog began to clear one day when Francis stopped by a wayside church. Then, as now, the Italian landscape raised churches as profusely as olives. The church named for St. Damian was one of many just outside the walls of Assisi. The ancient walls of the tiny building were crumbling with age and neglect. Francis looked constantly for places where he could be alone to pray, to beg to know God's will. San Damiano may have been the hundredth—or the thousandth—door he breached in his quest. The *Catholic Encyclopedia* has a terse but poetic way of telling the story: "Whilst Francis was praying before an ancient crucifix in the forsaken wayside chapel of St. Damian's below the town, he heard a voice saying: 'Go, Francis, and repair my house, which as you see is falling into ruin.'"

Though Francis had had many "visions" up to this point, they seem to have come in dreams, or a voice in his head, or even a nudge in a direction of thought. St. Bonaventure explains that, this time, it was different: "Francis was alone in the church and he was terrified at the sound of the voice." Even though he had pined and begged and waited for God's voice, Francis was stunned when it came. Thomas of Celano says that the message was so powerful, so clearly the one for which Francis had been waiting, that in time it "penetrated his heart." Francis abandoned his fear and embraced the ecstasy that followed.

So eager was Francis for this direction that his enthusiasm in following it was nearly comical. He plundered his father's shop and loaded his horse with all the cloth it could carry. He rode to nearby Foligno and sold the cloth—and his horse. He took the proceeds back to Assisi (presumably on foot) and presented them to the priest who ministered at poor San Damiano.

The priest was not quite as willing as Francis to throw caution to the wind. He recognized Francis and knew the money must be traceable to Pietro Bernardone—a man not known for his generosity. He refused the money, which Francis tossed onto a windowsill in disdain, but allowed Francis to stay with him and make such repairs to the little church as his soft-skinned hands would permit. Far from a mercenary gesture, the priest seems to have been trying to protect Francis from Pietro, who, he was certain, would not be pleased by this turn of events. The priest was right.

chapter
five

His Father's Son

If the young Francis thrived in the world of medieval Assisi, it was a trait he came by honestly. His father, Pietro, was the very image of the rising merchant class—a man who braved difficult journeys, managed a thriving business, and indulged his son whenever some new ambition came into view. While Pica was seen turning a blind eye when Francis's zeal for giving to the poor seemed a bit excessive, Pietro was nowhere to be found. He may have been on a business trip (these would typically take months), or perhaps he left the management of the household to his wife. By the time Francis holed up at San Damiano, though, the news made its way back home. Pietro was furious.

Pietro gathered a handful of men and went to San Damiano to retrieve what was his. Francis had heard that his father was en route and left the little church for a nearby cave. Thomas of Celano excuses what might seem to be cowardice by explaining that Francis was "new to the service of Christ" and "wished to avoid his father's anger." Francis, though, later accused himself of cowardice. After thirty days of living in a cave, subsisting on little food and water, racked with pain and confusion over his father's anger and the quick end to which his service of God seemed to have come, Francis resolved to face Pietro.

Francis was filthy and gaunt. Sleepless nights had left him looking haggard and ill. When he took the road back toward Assisi, the townspeople who had once crowned him king of revels were shocked at his appearance. Imagining that he must have gone mad, they pelted him with stones, mud, and insults. The clamor was so great that it reached the ears of Pietro. If Pietro had been angry before at the extent to which Francis failed to fulfill his promise, seeing his once-golden boy jeered at by the rabble enraged him. He rushed to the center of the crowd, not to rescue Francis, but to drag him home to a sterner justice. When the boy refused to respond to reason, Pietro tried threats. Threats gave way to blows which, in turn, gave way to chains.

The starving, tortured Francis was beaten, bound, and locked in a small, lightless room.

Somewhere in that cave outside Assisi, though, Francis had truly found God. His fear, confusion, and self-loathing were transformed into a still, quiet joy. This gave him the strength to head home once again, to endure the harassment of the town. It gave him the courage to withstand his father's anger and abuse. True, he was no longer setting stone upon stone at San Damiano as he thought he should, but he had found a new identity in God—an identity separate from doing. From that point forward, whatever he was doing or not doing, saying or not saying, he was serving God.

In his *Major Life of St. Francis*, St. Bonaventure explains what happened next:

> Shortly afterwards his father had to go away and his mother, who had never approved of her husband's action, loosed Francis' bonds and let him go free. She saw that there was no hope of breaking his inflexible determination. Francis gave thanks to God and went back where he had been before. When his father came home and failed to find him, he heaped abuse on his wife and

then went after Francis in a storm of rage; if he could not bring him home, at least he could drive him from the country. But God gave Francis courage and he went out to meet his father on his own accord and told him plainly that he was not afraid of ill-treatment or imprisonment, adding that for Christ's sake he would gladly endure any suffering. When his father realized that he could not hope to make him turn back, he concentrated on trying to recover his money, and when he eventually found it on the window-sill, his greed was satisfied and he calmed down a little.

Now that he had recovered his money, he arranged to have Francis brought before the bishop of the diocese, where he should renounce all his claims and return everything he had. In his genuine love for poverty, Francis was more than ready to comply and he willingly appeared before the bishop. There he made no delay—without hesitation, without hearing or saying a word—he immediately took off his clothes and gave them back to his father. Then it was discovered that he wore a hair-shirt under his fine clothes next to his skin. He even took off his trousers in his fervor and enthusiasm and stood there naked before them all. Then he said to his father, "Until now I called you my father, but from now on I can say without reserve, 'Our Father who art in heaven.' He is all my wealth and I place all my confidence in him." When the bishop heard this, he was amazed at his passionate fervor. He jumped to his feet and took Francis into his embrace, covering him with the cloak he was wearing, like the good man that he was. Then he told his servants to bring some clothes for him and they gave him an old tunic which belonged to one of the bishop's farmhands. Francis took it gratefully and drew a cross on it with his own hand with a piece of chalk, making it a worthy garment for a man who was crucified and a beggar. And so the servant of the most high King was left stripped of all that belonged to him, that he might follow the Lord whom he loved, who hung naked on the cross. He was armed with the cross, the means of salvation which would enable him to escape from a shipwrecked world.

Now that he was free from the bonds of all earthly desires in his disregard for the world, Francis left the town and sought out a place where he could be alone, without a care in the world. There in solitude and silence he would be able to hear God's secret revelations.

Then as he was walking through the forest joyfully singing in French and praising God, he was suddenly set upon by robbers. They threatened him and asked him who he was but he replied intrepidly with the prophetic words, "I am the herald of the great King." Then they beat him and threw him into a ditch full of snow, telling him, "Lie there, rustic herald of God." With that they made off and Francis jumped from the ditch, full of joy, and made the woods re-echo with his praise to the Creator of all.

None of Francis's biographers record any further meeting between Francis and his parents. Whatever pain Pica and Pietro must have experienced not merely by losing the company of this son, but by having been rejected by a son whose misbehavior they had accepted for so long, history does not record that Francis did anything to heal those wounds.

If there was any glory to be had in growing into his role as the dashing, witty son of Pietro Bernardone, Francis had found a greater glory. However destitute and pitiable it would make him, he would be the son of a greater Father.

The Gospel

After stripping himself naked before Bishop Guido, Francis clothed himself in the rags of a hermit. Having quieted the inner conflict spurred by his father's expectations, Francis returned to the church at San Damiano and set to performing the task God had given him. He set stone upon stone, begging building materials from passersby and the people of Assisi. When San Damiano had been rebuilt, Francis moved to the next tiny church, St. Peter. Again he begged stones for the church and bread to sustain himself. When St. Peter was restored, he moved to yet another—a little chapel called St. Mary of the Angels, which would one day be known as the Portiuncula. He still had not gone far from home; each of these little churches could be seen from most windows in Assisi.

The townspeople were perplexed. Here was that same hand-some man whose rich clothes put the nobility to shame, now dressed in rags. Here was that dashing would-be knight with his soft hands bare of weapons, inexpertly stacking stones. Here was that witty king of revels whose late-night songs were now hymns of praise. They may have thought he was crazy. Some might have decided that his brief military career and lengthy imprisonment were finally catching up with him. Some may even have thought that this was his longest, most elaborate practical joke yet. But everyone found him impossible to ignore.

In *Francis and His Brothers: A Popular History of the Franciscan Friars*, Dominic Monti explains how this lifestyle was understood by Francis and his bewildered former friends and neighbors:

> Francis's dramatic decision to break with his father and "leave the world" meant that he had become a kind of leper himself, forced to fashion a new existence on the margins of Assisi society. For the first year or two, he spent much of his time alone, devoting himself to prayer and repairing several small chapels in the rural areas around Assisi while continuing to minister among

the lepers. From the Church's perspective, Francis was a lay penitent hermit, one of many such freelance religious who were a prominent feature of life in central Italy. As such, he enjoyed the protection of Bishop Guido. It is ironic that this prelate, known to be an avaricious, litigious man intent on maintaining his rights and privileges, remained a faithful supporter and spiritual guide of Francis, who was so committed to reconciliation and peace.

But Francis's journey of "doing penance" was only just beginning. About two years later, in 1208, his life took a further turn as he recalled in his Testament, "when the Lord gave me brothers" and "revealed to me that I should live according to the form of the Holy Gospel." One day, two other citizens of Assisi, Bernard of Quintavalle, like Francis from an upper-middle-class family, and another man, known only as Peter, approached him, wishing to share his life. According to one early account, Francis suggested they seek direction from God, and so the three went up to Assisi, entered the Church of St. Nicholas on the town square and asked the priest if they might see the Gospel of Christ. The priest presented them with a missal; then Francis, following a popular religious practice for discerning God's will, paused to pray and then opened the book three times at random. Each time, their eyes fell on a Gospel passage that spoke of the radical renunciation to which Jesus called his followers: his invitation to the rich young man to sell everything he possessed and give the money to the poor (Mark 10:21), his demand that they deny themselves and take up their cross (Matthew 16:24), and his instructions to the apostles to take nothing for the journey as they went out to proclaim God's reign (Luke 9:3).

This was not a dream or a vision; it was not an inner voice. This was the Gospel. This was the very same book Francis had heard at least weekly, possibly daily. The book that for twelve hundred years had been what Christians—at first a daring few, soon all of Europe and beyond—built their lives upon. The book that still outsells every other. The Good News was not new news, but what Francis did with it was. He put it into practice.

Bonaventure tells us that these words had a galvanizing effect on Francis. "This is what I want," he cried. "This is what I long for with all my heart."

There and then he took off his shoes and laid aside his staff. He conceived a horror of money or wealth of any kind and he wore only one tunic, changing his leather belt for a rope. The whole desire of his heart was to put what he had heard into practice and conform to the rule of life given to the Apostles in everything.

From that day forward, Francis dressed himself in the poorest clothes he could find. Though ironic, it would not be unfair to suggest that humility had become a point of pride for him; whenever he passed someone clothed more poorly than himself, he'd give away a cloak or trade tunics. Ultimately he was dressed in a coarse brown tunic gathered with a simple cord—a tunic he patched and repatched and wore for the rest of his life.

chapter seven

Brothers

Bernard and Peter could not be separated from Francis. That same charisma that won him followers in revelry and war had only been magnified once Francis had found his true purpose. Though he felt he was only beginning to understand what God wanted from him, Francis allowed these men to join him. Rather than followers, as one might expect any guru to attract, Francis called them "brothers." He did not imagine that he could lead them to God, but he was joyous to have companions on his own journey.

The chapel Francis had most recently worked on, St. Mary of the Angels, was owned by a nearby Benedictine abbey. The land was virtually worthless and the Benedictines allowed Francis and his brothers to stay there in a small hut they had built next to the church. This was the origin of the term "Portiuncula"— "Little Portion." The brothers thought it best to stay outside the city and make their home with the outcasts—the beggars, the lepers, the madmen. They wanted to live on borrowed land, so they would not be "contaminated" by wealth. And, of course, they wanted a place to worship.

As more men joined their number, the contrast between their way of life and that of the ordinary citizens of Assisi became that much more noticeable. Those ordinary folk might have seemed wildly religious by today's standards. Social life revolved around the Church—the feasts of the liturgical year were not obscure practices, they were, quite literally, holidays. The few who could afford books of their own would own prayer books or copies of the Gospels. Even for the wealthy, life could be hard and short and everyone took salvation very seriously.

At the same time, what Francis was doing seemed, well, crazy. Who would beg, if it could be avoided? Who would dress in rags, when warm, beautiful clothes were at hand? Who would live among the poor and outcast, when once every respectable door in town had been opened to you? This behavior seemed suspicious, disreputable; it threatened an already shaky social structure with chaos.

Holding up the lifestyle of Francis and his brothers against the Gospel of Christ, it was easy to see that they were striving to follow it in every respect. If their practice had limits, they were working to perfect it. But then comparing their way of life to that of the average townspeople showed a vast gap. If there were any overlap, one could be sure the respectable townsfolk were doing their best to eliminate it.

If Francis was following Christ and the average person was striving to live in a manner as far from Francis's as possible, that could lead to only one logical—and very uncomfortable—conclusion. Taking the Gospel seriously meant living according to its words, just as Francis did. Everything the people of Assisi had learned about what it meant to live a good life had veered very far off course.

This contrast was, in part, responsible for the many men who were attracted to Francis's way of life. Some had been his friends in his "normal" life. Others were townsmen, peasants, even a knight. No matter what life these men had been leading, it was not a Christian life, they came to understand. It was a realization they might never have made if it had not been for Francis's example.

Of course, there is more than one way to live a Christian life. Francis and his brothers demonstrated that there are as many authentic vocations to follow Christ as there are Christians. While Francis had been living as a hermit, in time he and his followers took to heart the mission of the apostles. They lived both in and out of the world, but, as Monti explains, they changed the way they lived in it:

> ...laboring at the same jobs as other people, but using the good things of God's creation in such a way as not to deprive others of them. Although they dwelt down in the valley some distance from Assisi, they would trek back up into the city or to the leper hospices to work. There they practiced the trades they knew, but no longer for profit. Refusing to accept money as wages, they received only the necessities of life—food, clothing, and shelter—which they shared among themselves and with the poor. In this way, with no property to defend and no agenda of material gain, they were free to approach all people as equal in God's sight, worthy of attention and concern.

The brothers' preaching and example became an inspiration. Those who could, joined them; those who could not adopted their way of life as much as they could within the structure of their "ordinary" lives. In time, Francis and the brothers traveled throughout the region, preaching the Gospel in pairs, as Jesus had sent his disciples to do. Once they left the territory of Assisi, however, their work expanded beyond the borders controlled by the local bishop. If they wanted to spread the Gospel far and wide (and they did), they would need a higher authority.

Francis did not set out to establish a religious community. He wanted to pursue the lifestyle outlined in the Gospels. Strangely, despite the many religious orders and disciplines active at the time, none quite fit his vision of the Gospel life. Even within the wide world of the universal Church, Francis was doing something new.

The few Gospel precepts around which Francis had organized his life and those of his brothers were soon overwhelmed by detail. The Gospel advised poverty, but not everyone agreed on what poverty meant. Chastity and obedience had similar challenges. Then there were questions about what to wear, what to eat, when to fast, how and when to pray, and whether friars could own horses.

Francis convinced Pope Innocent III to formally approve his Gospel way of life, but the pontiff did so orally. In keeping with the informality of Francis's principles, this "rule" did not quite meet the legal litmus test. It would be many years (and several meetings, or "chapters" of the friars) before a written rule was sophisticated enough to meet with papal approval. This was approved in 1221.

This document still disappointed some of the friars. For some, it was still too simplistic. For others, it lacked the necessary precision to be an effective guide for the daily lives of the brothers. A "Second Rule" was approved by Pope Honorius III in 1223. It was very close in spirit to the First Rule and to those Gospel principles which had long guided Francis's life. It is the same rule that guides the Franciscan friars today.

chapter eight

Sisters

No story of Francis would be complete without some mention of St. Clare. Twelve years younger than Francis, this beautiful noblewoman was devoted to a life of celibacy and penance, much to the disappointment of her family who had hoped to marry her into money, power, or both. Her cousin Rufino, a knight, joined the friars and told Francis of her faith and piety. Rufino arranged for the two to meet.

Francis had adopted a radical lifestyle. Once Clare understood what he and his brothers had done, she proposed something even more radical—the same Gospel lifestyle, but for *women*. Women had taken religious vows before, true enough, but in a much more secure way. Much like the Benedictine monks, they enjoyed a certain level of security behind cloister walls. They were not merely physically secure from the prying eyes and impure intentions of men; they were financially secure as well. Young women brought their dowries with them into religious life, bolstering the community coffers against the cost of feeding and housing them.

What Clare proposed was a community of poor women, who would support themselves with manual labor and who would do so *out in the world*. Even Francis was taken aback by this. A community of women, yes; poverty and a Gospel lifestyle, maybe; but undefended chaste virgins roaming the countryside doing good? Against the harsh backdrop of the Middle Ages, that must have seemed an invitation to tragedy.

Undeterred by what seemed impossible, Clare resolved to take what steps she could toward a Franciscan lifestyle. She slipped out of the family palace one moonlit Palm Sunday night, escaped through the gates of the city and met Francis at the Portiuncula. She allowed her beautiful hair to be shorn and exchanged her fine clothing for the coarse tunic of a penitent.

One of the best sources we have on the life of Clare, the *Legend of Saint Clare the Virgin*, explains her family's reaction:

> …after the news reached her relatives, they condemned with a broken heart the deed and proposal of the virgin and, banding together as one, they ran to the place attempting to obtain what they could not. They employed violent force, poisonous advice and flattering promises, persuading her to give up such a worthless deed that was unbecoming to her class and without precedent in her family. But taking hold of the altar cloths, she bared her tonsured head, maintaining that she would in no way be torn away from the service of Christ.

Having succeeded in winning his first sister, Francis was faced with a problem. He did not know what to do with her. She couldn't stay with the brothers—that would be scandalous. And returning to her family while he thought of something was not an option—that bridge had been thoroughly burned. He found a nearby convent that would take her in—San Paolo delle Abbadesse. She could not enter as a nun, though. Without a dowry, she entered as a servant, to the profound disgrace of her family.

Within a short time, the resourceful Francis worked with Bishop Guido on an alternative. Clare and the women who followed her (most from her own social class) were housed at the church at San Damiano, where Francis had first heard that voice from the cross. These "Poor Ladies" devoted themselves to prayer and caring for the sick and supported themselves with their own hands. It wasn't exactly the life Clare wanted—both Francis and the pope were afraid to allow the women to vow themselves to utter poverty and itinerancy. It was an important start, though, for Clare, for the community she would one day organize under her own Rule (the first written by a woman), and for Francis, who had learned yet another way of following Christ.

The women's branch (or "second order") of Franciscanism paved the way for yet another: the third order, composed of laypeople who wanted a Gospel lifestyle but could not join the brothers or sisters for some reason—usually because of family obligations. Francis knew that the Gospel was not just for those who could abandon a "normal" life for the cloister or monastery. The Good News was meant for everyone. One contemporary witness of the two communities described them in these terms:

In this region, many well-to-do secular people have left all things for Christ and fled the world. They are called "Lesser Brothers" and "Lesser Sisters." They are held in great reverence by the Lord Pope and the Cardinals…. During the day the brothers go into the cities and villages giving themselves over to the active life in order to gain others; at night, however, they return to their hermitage or solitary places to devote themselves to contemplation. The women dwell together near the cities in various hospices, accepting nothing, but living by the work of their hands.

It is hard to know when—or whether—Francis realized it, but to the rest of the world it was becoming clear. That call from the cross in San Damiano to "rebuild my church" was not just a plea for those four stone walls, but a command to recall the entire Church back to the life of Christ. By his example, his preaching, his brothers and sisters, Francis of Assisi rebuilt the Catholic Church.

Conclusion

The Gospel of John concludes with the words, "But there are also many other things that Jesus did; if every one of them were written down, I suppose that the world itself could not contain the books that would be written." Francis conformed his life to Christ's in this way, just as he tried to do in every other.

Perhaps the story most helpful for our time is that of Francis's visit to the sultan. Franciscan friar Jack Wintz sums up the visit:

> In the year 1219, while Christian Crusaders were engaged in bloody combat with Muslim forces, St. Francis traveled to Damietta, Egypt, where he met with Sultan Malik al-Kamil, the Muslim leader.
>
> Convinced that violence and war marked the wrong path, Francis determined to engage in peaceful dialogue with the sultan and with the larger Muslim world. When he gained entrance to the sultan's camp, he fearlessly tried to persuade his Muslim host that Christ was the true path to salvation.

Although the sultan was not about to change religions, he admired Francis's enthusiasm and courage, and listened respectfully to him. Francis also showed a deep respect for his Muslim brother. The sultan offered gifts to Francis and saw to it that he was given safe passage back to the Christian camp. As they parted, according to one account, the sultan said to Francis, "Pray for me that God may reveal to me the law and the faith that is more pleasing to him."

As for the many stories beyond the scope of this little introduction, all have one theme in common. No matter the circumstances, Francis continually worked to discover God's will and to live each day more perfectly than the last. We may never speak to the birds, have heavenly visions, or change the course of history, but we can still follow his example in that respect. It was this continual joy at the newness of life, at the fresh beginning each moment brings, that saw Francis through to the end of his life, when he said, "Brothers, let us begin again, for up to now, we have done nothing."

Bibliography

Bartoli, Marco. *Saint Clare: Beyond the Legend,* Sister Frances Teresa Downing, O.S.C., trans. (Cincinnati: St. Anthony Messenger Press, 2010).

Bodo, Murray. *Francis: The Journey and the Dream* (Cincinnati: Franciscan Media, 2011).

_____. *The Simple Way: Meditations on the Words of Saint Francis* (Cincinnati: St. Anthony Messenger Press, 2009).

Carroll, Kathleen M. *A Franciscan Christmas* (Cincinnati: St. Anthony Messenger Press, 2010).

Chesterton, G.K. "St. Francis of Assisi," in *The Collected Works of G.K. Chesterton, Volume 2* (San Francisco: Ignatius, 1987).

Delio, Ilia, O.S.F. *Compassion: Living in the Spirit of St. Francis* (Cincinnati: St. Anthony Messenger Press, 2011).

Englebert, Omer. *St. Francis of Assisi: A Biography* (Ann Arbor, Mich.: Servant, 1979).

Habig, Marion V., ed. *Saint Francis of Assisi: Omnibus of Sources* (Cincinnati: St. Anthony Messenger Press, 2008).

Monti, Dominic V., o.f.m. *Francis and His Brothers: A Popular History of the Franciscan Friars* (Cincinnati: St. Anthony Messenger Press, 2009).

Saint Sing, Susan. *Francis and the San Damiano Cross: Meditations on Spiritual Transformation* (Cincinnati: St. Anthony Messenger Press, 2007).

Thompson, Augustine. *Francis of Assisi: A New Biography* (New York: Cornell University Press, 2012).